P9-CSA-931

Lebanon

by Thomas Persano

Consultant: Marjorie Faulstich Orellana, PhD
Professor of Urban Schooling
University of California, Los Angeles

New York, New York

Credits

Cover, © Richard Yoshida/Shutterstock and © gradyreese/iStock; TOC, © Diego Fiore/Shutterstock; 4, © Anna Omelchenko/Panther Media GmbH/Alamy; 5T, © Henryk Sadura/Shutterstock; 5B, © Joerg Boethling/Alamy; 7, © Milonk/Dreamstime; 8, © Viktor Molnar/Shutterstock; 9T, © Images by Itani/Alamy; 9B, © OSTILL/iStock; 10T, © Andyworks/iStock; 10B, © Uros Poteko/Alamy; 11, © Bartosz Budrewicz/Shutterstock; 12, © De Agostini Picture Library/Bridgeman Images; 13T, © Jordi Camí/AGE Fotostock; 13B, © Radiokafka/Shutterstock; 14, © Monikamonia/Dreamstime; 15T, © Geoff Dunlop/Alamy; 15B, © Rihan/AP Images; 16, © minemero/iStock; 17T, © Diego Fiore/Shutterstock; 17B, © char abumansoor/Alamy; 18–19, © Hans Münch/Panther Media GmbH/Alamy; 20, © Alan Gignouz/Dreamstime; 21, © Joel Carillet/iStock; 22T, © alpaksoy/iStock; 22B, © ALLEKO/iStock; 23, © margouillat photo/Shutterstock; 24, © HomoCosmicos/iStock; 25T, © f8grapher/Alamy; 25B, © Kobby Dagan/Shutterstock; 26, © Jamal Saidi/Reuters/Newscom; 27T, © Alan Gignoux/Dreamstime; 27B, © Muhammad Hamed/Reuters/Newscom; 28L, © Eliane Haykal/Alamy; 28–29, © Craig Stennett/Alamy; 30T, © Siempreverde22/Dreamstime and © asafta/iStock; 30B, © Ed Kashi/VII/Redux Pictures; 31 (T to B), © diplomedia/Shutterstock, © Rihan/AP Images, © Geoff Dunlop/Alamy, © diak/Shutterstock, © dkaranouh/iStock, and © Beautiful Landscape/Shutterstock; 32, © rook76/Shutterstock.

Publisher: Kenn Goin
Senior Editor: Joyce Tavolacci
Creative Director: Spencer Brinker
Design: Debrah Kaiser
Photo Researcher: Thomas Persano

Library of Congress Cataloging-in-Publication Data
Names: Persano, Thomas, author.
Title: Lebanon / by Thomas Persano.
Description: New York, New York : Bearport Publishing, [2019] | Series:
   Countries we come from | Includes bibliographical references and index.
Identifiers: LCCN 2018014547 (print) | LCCN 2018024604 (ebook) |
   ISBN 9781684027316 (Ebook) | ISBN 9781684026852 (library)
Subjects: LCSH: Lebanon—Juvenile literature.
Classification: LCC DS80 (ebook) | LCC DS80 .P475 2019 (print) |
   DDC 956.92—dc23
LC record available at https://lccn.loc.gov/2018014547

Copyright © 2019 Bearport Publishing Company, Inc. All rights reserved. No part of this publication may be reproduced in whole or in part, stored in any retrieval system, or transmitted in any form or by any means, electronic, mechanical, photocopying, recording, or otherwise, without written permission from the publisher.

For more information, write to Bearport Publishing Company, Inc., 45 West 21st Street, Suite 3B, New York, New York 10010. Printed in the United States of America.

10 9 8 7 6 5 4 3 2 1

Contents

Beautiful

ANCIENT

WARM

Lebanon is a small country in western Asia.

It's located on the Mediterranean Sea.

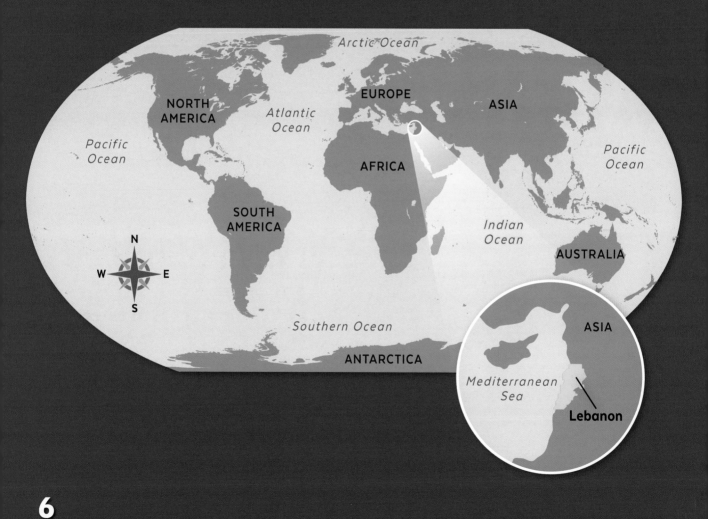

Over six million people live in Lebanon.

Lebanon has soaring mountains.

Between the mountains lies a huge valley.

There, farmers grow fruits and vegetables.

grape farmer

Cedar trees grow in the mountains. A cedar tree appears on Lebanon's flag.

Many interesting animals live in Lebanon.

Birds called kestrels fly high in the sky.

kestrel

Golden jackals make their home in the countryside.

The rock hyrax is a small, furry animal. It lives in rocky areas in Lebanon.

In ancient times, the Phoenician (fuh-NEE-shun) people lived in Lebanon.

They often traveled by sea.

They built large cities, such as Tyre.

Phoenician writing

The alphabet we use today comes from the Phoenicians.

Since the time of the Phoenicians, Lebanon has had many rulers.

The Romans and Ottomans once controlled the land.

Later, the French ruled.

the remains of a Roman city

Finally, in 1943, the country became **independent**.

Since then, Lebanon has been affected by many wars.

From 1975 to 1990, there was a **civil war** inside the country. Many people died.

The **capital** of Lebanon is Beirut.

Nearly two million people live there.

The city is located on the coast.

People enjoy strolling along the sea.

Beirut has a large market. It's called *Souk el Tayeb*, which means "good market" in Arabic.

North of Beirut is Jeita.

This town is famous for its caves.

Visitors come to see amazing **rock formations**.

One cave in Jeita has a huge **stalactite**. It's 27 feet (8.2 m) long!

stalactite

Most people in Lebanon speak Arabic.
This is how you say *hello* in Arabic:

Marhaba (MAR-ha-bah)

This is how you say *thank you*:

Chokran (SHOW-kran)

Many Lebanese people also speak French.

شارع ذو طابع تراثي
**Rue
à Caractère Traditionnel**

a sign in Arabic and French

There's lots of delicious food in Lebanon!

Kibbe is a tasty dish made with ground lamb.

tabbouleh

Parsley, tomato, and wheat salad is called *tabbouleh*.

Most meals are served with pita bread.

People often eat meze, which is a group of small side dishes.

Religion is a big part of life in Lebanon.

The two main religions are Islam and Christianity.

Muslims practice Islam in mosques.

mosque

Christians worship in churches.

inside a church

a Druze woman

Druze is another important religion in Lebanon. It's related to Islam.

What do people do for fun in Lebanon?

Many people love to ski!

Swimming is also a favorite activity.

Families flock to beaches on the coast.

Soccer is the most popular sport in the country!

Clap your hands!

In Lebanon, people dance the *dabke*. (DAB-kee)

First, dancers line up.

Then, they stomp their feet and jump!

A drummer plays music for dabke dancers.

Fast Facts

Capital city: Beirut

Population of Lebanon: Over 6 million

Main languages: Arabic and French

Money: Lebanese pound

Major religions: Islam and Christianity

Neighboring countries: Israel and Syria

Cool Fact:
A Lebanese wedding often lasts for three days!

capital (KAP-uh-tuhl) a city where a country's government is based

civil war (SIV-il WOR) a war between people of the same country

independent (in-di-PEN-duhnt) free from outside control

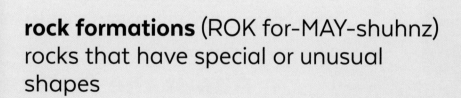

rock formations (ROK for-MAY-shuhnz) rocks that have special or unusual shapes

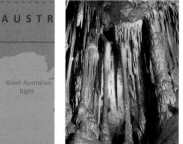

stalactite (stuh-LAK-tite) an icicle-shaped rock that hangs from the roof of a cave

31

Index

Read More

Englar, Mary. *Lebanon (A Question and Answer Book).* Minneapolis, MN: Capstone (2007).

Stewart, James. *Lebanon (Countries in Crisis).* Vero Beach, FL: Rourke (2008).

Learn More Online

To learn more about Lebanon, visit
www.bearportpublishing.com/CountriesWeComeFrom

About the Author

Thomas Persano lives in New York City. He has never been to Lebanon but would like to explore all its ancient sites one day.